"... a new voice that speaks in an extraordinarily clear and deceptively simple way of the mighty things of the soul many of us are too busy to notice. I am grateful for this book, which compels my attention and feeds both mind and soul."

The Rev. Professor Peter Gomes
Professor of Christian Morals
Harvard University
Cambridge, Massachusetts

"Pat Youngdahl has written a beautiful and stirring book—painful, lyrical, crushing, and wonder-filled. You will laugh and cry and sigh and come out stronger and more hopeful."

Mary Ann Lundy
Former Deputy Secretary General
World Council of Churches
Geneva, Switzerland

"I have waited for this book from deep in my soul. Here it is now just when we need it most, to challenge the church to become the welcoming inclusive place it is meant to be."

The Rev. Dr. Jane Adams Spahr
Director, That All May Freely Serve
Rochester, New York

Continued on page 119

Blessings on your journey...
Pat Youngdahl

SUBVERSIVE DEVOTIONS

A JOURNEY INTO DIVINE PLEASURE AND POWER

PAT YOUNGDAHL

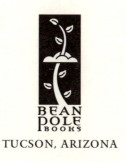

TUCSON, ARIZONA

Copyright © 2003 by Pat Youngdahl

Published by
BeanPole Books
An imprint of Harren Communications, LLC
4134 E. Hawthorne St.
Tucson, AZ 85711
888-815-5961

All rights reserved. This book may not be reproduced in whole or in part by any means whatsoever without written permission from the publisher, except by a reviewer who may quote brief passages. No part of this book may be stored in a retrieval system or transmitted in any form or by any means, electronic, mechanical, photocopied, recorded, or other, without written permission from the publisher.

Book and cover design by mindthwack inc.
ISBN   0-9667359-5-1
Printed in the United States of America on acid-free paper

9   8   7   6   5   4   3   2   1

To all who dare

one step, then the next, on the journey into love.

No one can take your place.

FOREWORD

OUR DEVOTIONS BRING OUR MOST profound yearnings into the world, whether through the spiritual practice of prayer and meditation, or through the daily pleasure of loving those to whom we are committed, or through the continuing struggle for justice. Yet, how do we cherish these desires and commitments if they are rejected by those around us?

After all, though we often undertake our devotions in solitude, they are fundamentally social acts. The devotions we enact are meaningful to us partly because they connect us with communities—such as neighborhoods, congregations, workplaces, schools, friendship networks, and social movements—that help us make sense of the world. Our communities teach us particular ways to answer our questions and can offer us strong support. But what happens when our community determines that our loves are not acceptable to them, that our justice is not their justice, that our lives are somehow unworthy? Rather than sustaining life and love, does enacting devotion in such a setting require us to sustain harm?

This is the question faced by all too many people in our world: gay and lesbian people whose loves are denied or denounced; people of color who contend with racism in U.S. society and sometimes in their congregations; women who are daily assaulted by sexism; people whose dignity is damaged by poverty. Sometimes communities provide such people a source of solace and strength, or a context for healing and wholeness, or the wisdom of social critique and the power of struggle.

But all too often, it is the very communities to which one might turn—for help, for faith, for courage—that inflict the most harm.

We are loath to utter this thought. Our situations are rarely clear cut. As we struggle for justice in an imperfect world, our communities may offer us very mixed messages. They may mingle solace with sacrifice; they may tell us that they love us even as they deny important aspects of our lives. So, how do we practice our devotions even when the support of others fails us?

The gift Pat Youngdahl offers us in *Subversive Devotions* is an intimate view of her own journey—a journey through which she grew to trust her love for herself and the world rather than submit to the dictates of hatred and injustice. She became a scholar of rhetoric, she tells us, "partly because I wanted to figure out how to extricate myself from the oppressions of the church while treasuring its gifts." She recounts how, in faith, she affirmed the deepest devotions of her life; she shows how, faced with hostility from both society and church, she learned to embrace subversive work—to "untangle love from domination."

This is a subversive book. It encourages each of us to extricate ourselves from oppression without giving up on the gifts of liberation. It fosters our power to acknowledge the harm done to us, to be angry when we have suffered injustice, and to honor the wisdom of our lives. It asks us to take up hope, a radical hope that "does not pretend to know it all," a hope that allows us "to proceed as if our lives matter and as if every one of us can contribute in irreplaceable ways to the shared well-being that we have not, after all, forgotten how to desire."

Such a journey requires courage, yet it also abounds with blessings of comfort and delight. Pat speaks to us of "the grace of being loved, of becoming our truest, bravest selves in response to divine gifts we cannot know how to anticipate." She shares with us her laughter "ancient and new, foolish and ecstatic." She shakes her head over the puzzles of existence, and she embraces divine love in times of challenge. Finally, she invites us to love the world with "tenderness and power," to bring to the world "our questions and stories, our enlivening gifts," to grieve our losses together so that we may fully experience our joys, and, yes, to bring our own vision and passion to the practice of subversive devotions.

Janet R. Jakobsen, Ph.D.
Director, Center for Research on Women
Associate Professor of Women's Studies
Barnard College
New York, New York

INTRODUCTION

WE ARE ALWAYS AND EVERYWHERE AT our devotions. In some moments we are especially attentive to them. When we light a candle, kiss a photograph, scatter a handful of ashes, enter a voting booth, or whisper a prayer, it is easy to catch sight of ourselves enacting our beliefs and desires. But usually we are not so aware. We move through most ordinary hours without recognizing that here, too, or perhaps here even more, since indeed we are not watching so closely, we perform the devotions by which we make sense of the world and give body to what is happening in our hearts.

Writing these pages, I made a journey into love. Entry by entry, I opened space for my soul to meet with divine presence even as

I faced the world's hostility to the devotions that bring wholeness to my life. I give thanks for that first summer morning when I sat down here at my desk, felt a breeze float in through the screen door, soft on my skin, and went out by faith into this writing. I wanted to comprehend how my embrace of divine love had led to such a time of challenge. I was ready to find out what would become of my intimacy with Jesus if I dared to love the world, including my life, with increasing pleasure and power.

At every turn, I drew courage from the community of *mujerista*[1], womanist, and other feminist theologians who are engaged in profoundly liberating work around the world. I am thankful most especially to Rita Nakashima Brock, for showing us how to heal violence at its roots, in our broken hearts[2]; to Ada María Isasi-Díaz, for calling us to transform social structures so that "nobody will be diminished"[3]; to Elisabeth Schüssler Fiorenza, for illuminating the ethics of scripture interpretation in relation to the survival and freedom of all[4], and to Delores Williams, for her celebration of the *life* of Jesus as the center for Christian spiritual practice[5]—with Delores, I want to live!

I rejoice that the life-loving purposes of this work have been furthered by the generous support of a Jacob K. Javits Fellowship; the Johnnie Raye Harper Award and the David Patrick Memorial Award, both from the English Department at the University of Arizona; the Jean Colton Fellowship for feminist spiritual writing; and a grant from the Amazon Foundation, an agency pursuing the well-being of women and girls in Southern Arizona.

I am tremendously happy to thank, as well, the loved ones who have inspired me in the struggle to stay with this writing, especially Banana Mae, our cat, for her wild, tender spiritual presence; Maggie, our collie, for taking me outdoors for long, ecstatic walks in every kind of weather; Twisp, our tarantula, for bursting out of her old skin each spring and reminding us to keep on growing; Catherine Harold, my editor, for the magic of her sparking me to discover what would otherwise go unsaid; Tilly Warnock, for the way we believe in each other; Tom Miller, for celebrating the writer in me; Mary Caravetta, for her undaunted embrace of life and laughter; Bob Kafes, for the courage we inspire in each other for seeking to heal the world; John Warnock, for our comradeship in the vocation of writing; Janet Jakobsen, for our adventures in activism and hope; Mary Carol Schaedel, for reminding me that rest and play are part of being creative; Ben Youngdahl, my nephew, for the stories we write together; Sandy Szelag, for sharing her wisdom as I learn to dwell in the heart; Deborah Flemister Mullen, for the treasure of our friendship through the years; Kelly Kurtz, for how we call each other forth into the sacred; and Michal McKenzie, for the sweet, strong blessings of our every day, and for the wondrous gift of her company as we keep saying yes to life and love.

Pat Youngdahl
Tucson, Arizona
Springtime 2002

Notes

1. *Mujerista* practices of scriptural interpretation and spirituality arise from the lives and reflections of Hispanic women as they engage in the struggle for racial, cultural, sexual, and economic justice. Womanist perspectives emerge from the living and theorizing of African American women engaged in this liberation struggle. The term "feminist" as I use it here sometimes refers to the work of Asian, Native American, European, and other women at work in this global movement, and sometimes it is a shorthand term to include everyone who is struggling toward the liberation of all people from patriarchal structures and processes.

2. Rita Nakashima Brock, scholar, theologian, and activist, has elaborated this insight in her *Journeys By Heart: A Christology of Erotic Power*, and in *Proverbs of Ashes: Violence, Redemptive Suffering, and the Search for What Saves Us*, written with Rebecca Ann Parker.

3. Ada María Isasi-Díaz, Co-Director of the Hispanic Institute of Theology at Drew University Theological School, has articulated this vision in her *En La Lucha: A Hispanic Women's Liberation Theology*, and in her "La Palabra de Dios en Nosotras—

The Word of God in Us," in *Searching the Scriptures: A Feminist Introduction*, edited by Elisabeth Schüssler Fiorenza.

4. Elisabeth Schüssler Fiorenza, the first woman president of the Society of Biblical Literature (1987) and the Krister Stendahl Professor of Divinity at Harvard Divinity School, has shown the liberating effects of interpreting Christian traditions from a rhetorical framework in her *But She Said: Feminist Practices of Biblical Interpretation*, and in her introduction to *Searching the Scriptures: A Feminist Introduction*.

5. Delores Williams, Paul Tillich Professor of Theology and Culture at Union Theological Seminary in New York City, has demonstrated the ethical significance of this perspective in her *Sisters in the Wilderness: The Challenge of Womanist God-Talk*, and in her "Black Women's Surrogacy Experience and the Christian Notion of Redemption," in *After Patriarchy: Feminist Transformations of the World Religions*, edited by Paula M. Cooey.

SUBVERSIVE DEVOTIONS

ON THE BUS

MY FALLING IN LOVE WITH GOD BEGAN on a bus rolling southwest from the green July of my hometown near Chicago, setting off toward the Ghost Ranch retreat center in Abiquiu, New Mexico. I sat between Kim and Dorothy, my two best friends, surrounded by twenty other junior high kids from Elmhurst Presbyterian Church. We three had chosen a seat right over one of the back tires, so whenever there was a bump, we flew a little.

Every now and then someone started up a song, and I would hear the voices rise and swirl around me with tales of loving mountains and rolling hills, firesides and daffodils; finding God's grace ready and sweet in every danger, toil, and snare; or

I

walking with Jesus through the lonesome valley and then down by the riverside to shake hands around the world.

My ears had never heard stories like these. My family didn't go to church. I signed up for the trip because Kim and Dorothy asked me and it sounded like fun— riding horses, hiking canyons, sneaking around after dark in church basements, climbing ladders up into cliff houses and down into kivas at Mesa Verde National Park. I didn't know how to expect a spiritual adventure. But there we were on the open road, in motion toward places we didn't know yet, except to yearn for—and singing of God! We slid our window down. The wind lifted my hair. Even when we weren't going over a bump, my soul flew a little.

BIRD BATH

TODAY WHEN I ANSWERED THE TEA-kettle's whistle, I saw out the back window a bird I didn't know. It stood on the edge of the birdbath, looking uncertain. The early sun on its scarlet crest had flashed at the corner of my eye. A cardinal? Not enough red. A female? A pyrrhuloxia, maybe? I ran for my binoculars and got back in time to see the bird stick one foot in the water up to its ankle, then pull back. I focused. Brilliant red streaks were mingled with haphazard patches of brown and buff. An orange bill emerged from a shiny black frame. A cardinal, then, for sure. A young male in transition toward the marvel of his full-fledged beauty.

I remember the voices of cardinals

sounding from the trees in our neighbor-hood through the years of my growing up. I heard them as I woke, or as I walked to school, or as I rounded third base after cracking a long fly ball into the bushes at the back of the field where we kids played. *Cheer, cheer, cheer!* those cardinals called to me. Or other times, as if shaking their heads over the puzzles of their existence as I sometimes do over mine, they murmured *Birds, birds, birds, birds, birds.*

This morning's cardinal jumped up into the oak tree when another bird arrived, a starling who bathed with abandon. When it left, the cardinal came back to the water's edge, looked around, and waded in. He dipped and shook a couple of times, still not at all sure, then flew back into the oak, frowzy and dripping, hopping a bit franti-cally from branch to branch, wondering, it seemed to me, *How do I get dry?*

VESPERS

AT SUPPER ON THE FIRST NIGHT OF OUR trip to Abiquiu, the Reverend Doctor Clare Tallman, who was every bit of all that, with white hair, too, and who soon taught us to write our own thoughts in the margins of our Bibles, announced that vespers would start in the library at seven o'clock. I showed up at the last minute, embarrassed and scared. What was a vesper? How would I know what to do? There I sat, telling myself that a somber silence would no doubt be enough to get me through, when I noticed with a jolt that a prayer was on its way around the circle and that when it got to me, I was supposed to do something with it, find a way somehow to get it into my mouth and then out again so that it could proceed to the next person's.

I decided to listen more deeply. People were saying thanks for things. Ordinary things. Things that had happened during the day. Thanks that we got to swim in the pool at this college, someone said. Thanks for when we stopped to eat ice cream. Thanks for the sun on all those cornfields we drove through. Thanks that I get to go on this trip with my friends.

I have no idea what I said when my turn came. What stayed with me was my happiness that this meditation on our day, this shared enjoyment, this improvisation arising from our many voices, could be prayer. At the time I didn't think in terms of theological implications, but my heart took note... God likes to hear our real voices. God cares about the details of our daily lives. God values our pleasure. Through all these years, whatever I have read or heard about divine presence, I have understood in this light. "God is love," our ministers preached, and I believed it. "Jesus calls us not servants, but friends," they proclaimed, and I knew what they meant.

BAPTISM

ON A BRIGHT DECEMBER MORNING, AT fourteen years old, I presented myself for baptism at the Elmhurst Presbyterian Church. My mom and dad visited the congregation that day, along with my great aunt, Linnea Youngdahl Langenberg, a fourth grade teacher in Chicago and a Swedish Lutheran who went to church every Sunday and often drove out to our house afterward for dinner. Beforehand, in the narthex, she gave me a book of prayers with a bright red cover and the inscription, "With love and all good wishes," written with festive red ink in her elegant hand.

I was nervous. My friends had all been baptized as infants. My prayer at the moment was that I would not trip on my way to or from the font. Reverend Jensen, who taught the confirmation class, had promised to meet me up there. He had opened our eyes to the very different audiences, purposes, and messages of the four gospel writers. On Saturday mornings, he drove several of us into Chicago so we could tutor grade-school students in math and language arts at Erie Neighborhood House. When I got to the font, Reverend Jensen in his black robe said the water was changed over "from a common to a sacred use," dipped his hand in, and let a few drops fall onto my head.

Next thing I knew, I was back in my seat, the sermon was over, and we in the ninth grade confirmation class were taking communion for the first time. Kim and Dorothy and I sat shoulder to shoulder in the front pew, giggling a little as we passed the silver plate adorned with uniform cubes of crustless bread. We got serious when the grape juice came around, doing our best to keep from tipping the tiny glass cups and spilling purple all over our white dresses.

One night after choir practice not long after, my new friend Sylvie and I slipped down the stairs behind the sanctuary into the dark and kissed. It was a baptism somewhat different from the sprinkling I had received in the chancel above. This time, I was drenched. I hadn't had the slightest notion how to hope for such a thing. But there we were. Alone on the landing, the exit light glowing down the hall. Her fingertips on my neck, in my hair. My lips brushing her cheek, finding her mouth.

The church was across from our high school. Its doors were unlocked during the day. Sylvie and I carried on in every corner of that building—the chilly bathroom, the crowded mop closet, the sacristy laced with the fragrance of candles, the choir loft warm with the orange and red of afternoon sun pouring through stained glass.

Looking back now, I see I was practicing what they preached. God so loves the world. The Word becomes flesh. You prepare a table before me in the presence of my enemies. You anoint my head with oil. My cup overflows. I will not leave you desolate. I will come to you. And then, waking every nerve in my soul and body, there she was. I knew God when I tasted her. My church had taught me well.

SOFT EARLY MORNINGS

OFTEN ON SOFT EARLY MORNINGS LIKE this, as light plays across the purple-gray slants of the Tucson Mountains, I return to myself as a very young child being astounded by the sun falling through the leaves of the trees around our house and landing warm on my skin where I sat in the grass below. For a long time, I had no words for the blessedness of such moments, but even way back then, my body was thankful.

ROOM TO BREATHE

NOT UNTIL COLLEGE DID I FIRST TRIP OVER Christian tradition's ongoing argument, present from the start, about what it means to have faith. It happened during my one and only visit to the Twin City Bible Church in Champaign-Urbana, early in my first semester at the University of Illinois. I was lonesome. I missed my old friends. When a second-year student, a woman I had known in the youth group back home, called and invited me to join her for worship at "TCBC" on Sunday evening, I was pleased. The words "Bible Church" had no associations for me. As far as I knew, a church was a church—a place to connect with God, learn about love, and make sense of life.

Yet as worship at TCBC unfolded, I felt

increasingly troubled, in danger, angry. I couldn't figure out what was wrong. The minister smiled often. But I didn't trust him. From here I can see that I was visiting a culture very different from the one in which I had come to faith. I had never before heard anyone suggest that "our Lord" had "died for me" in order to "accomplish the will of the Father." This minister made that claim repeatedly, his vehemence underscoring the not-quite-spoken threat that we had better respond now, with fervor, and in the ways he was prescribing—or else. By the end of that service, the last thing on earth I wanted was for Jesus to be "Lord of my life." My body wanted out of there. I was finding it hard to breathe.

Soon after, I looked up "Presbyterian" in the yellow pages and took myself to a service at the McKinley Presbyterian Church just off campus. Being full of professors and students, it wasn't just like my church back in Elmhurst, but before worship was over, I felt at home. Here as there, I had breathing room, space to wonder. Now faith could again be about walking with Jesus into joy and justice—and I could once more take up my part in the work of knowing and loving God.

SACRED TABLE

WHEN I WALK THE FEW BLOCKS FROM our house to the university, ready to teach, I often end up thinking about the mentors who have helped and inspired me. There are so many—I have been wondrously blessed over all these years, beginning early, at York High School, where I learned so much from my teachers in history, civics, and English. But this morning, it was Achsah Guibbory who came to mind, my favorite literature professor at Illinois. She guided my growth in creativity and intellect as I wrote my senior honors thesis, "The Motif of the Stranger in the Short Stories of Bernard Malamud." When we finished our work together that April, she asked me to her home and cooked me lunch. Just the two of us sat down at her kitchen table to eat salad, quiche, and bread. We talked of the springtime, of our dreams for the future. Achsah was so *herself*. Her happiness has carried me over many roads and still gives me strength.

SPIRITUAL FORMATION

PROFESSOR DALE JOHNSON, NO MATTER how he tried, could not get his lectures to end before the bell. Even after it rang, he needed a few minutes to make a landing. I didn't mind. By that time he would have launched the class four centuries into the past, ushered us into the Protestant Reformation, and piloted us through the clouds of some stormy theological debate, like the one between Luther and Zwingli about how divine love is present for believers in communion bread and wine.

Dale would put down the chalk, dust off his fingers, pick up the clock from his desk, and shake his head with a shy smile. My pages would be filled—with lecture notes, mostly, but also with my own leaps and weavings, scrawled in the margins, enclosed with boxes, and fastened with lines to the place in my notes where they came to me, so that they seemed to float out from the orderly borders of my paragraphs like so many kites.

This creativity, this ecstasy, this *salvation* took place as well when I heard our other professors lecture during my time at Vanderbilt Divinity School. I had been drawn to divinity school by my yearning to be intimate with God. The psalmist's prayer spoke for me: "As a deer longs for flowing streams, so my soul longs for you, O God." My professors were an answer to this prayer. They did their work, and in their presence, I did mine, and through our interchange, I felt the delight, the awakening, the expansion of my soul.

During my second year, I did a ministry internship at Nashville's Trinity Presbyterian

Church, where Dale belonged. That Fall, he and I taught a class together there on H. Richard Niebuhr's *Christ and Culture*. He encouraged my teaching and writing, and as my official school advisor, asked me whether I was sure I wanted to be a minister rather than a theology professor. For several weeks, I searched myself. Yes, I was sure.

One Sunday morning not long after, I went into the pulpit with a sermon I worried Dale would think was nowhere near intellectual enough and ridiculously down to earth. I spoke about the grace of being loved, of becoming our truest, bravest selves in response to divine gifts we cannot know how to anticipate. Dale came over after the benediction, his blue choir robe tossed over his arm, his eyes shining, and told me what had happened in his soul as he listened to me preach.

COMING ALIVE

A SIX-YEAR-OLD BOY AT THE FIRST Presbyterian Church of Itasca, Illinois, where I did a summer internship after my first year at Vanderbilt used to call me "the one who does the words on Sunday morning." That sanctuary had huge, old-fashioned windows. First thing each Sunday I would undo the locks and open those windows wide so that the breezes could come in for worship. In the last sermon I preached there, I talked about the many firsts of becoming a pastor—how frightened and moved I had felt as I preached the first sermon, taught the first class, walked home through a mist of warm rain after my first time of being with someone dying. None of this came easy for me, but I wanted to spend the rest of my life like that—getting wet, learning to love, coming alive.

LAGUNA BEACH

I PRAYED FOR LOVE THIS MORNING AS I stood at the edge of the water, watching the waves turn an utterly inconceivable shade of green just before they crested and plunged forward and thundered in, each one doing an irrepressible, unrepeatable drum solo before its final glide toward my feet. They say never to turn your back, and I hadn't. I saw it coming. I'd been figuring my distance with skill and backpedaling in time to keep my clothes entirely dry. Then, a little like the impossible, sudden tidal wave that visits my dreams, where I am thrilled and know it's imprudent, know I should race for safety, but don't, one wave just rose and rose, and what I did was look, not really believing, until it was too late. I turned to run but was knocked from my feet and carried in. I skinned my knees and hands on wet sand as water surged over me, then got my feet under me and pumped hard, stumbling against the sweep of the undertow. As soon as I made it, my laughter came, ancient and new, foolish and ecstatic. My shorts and shirt clung to me. The breeze swirled. I tasted salt, saw the pink-purple flowers through foamy droplets on my glasses, and felt for my baseball cap, the one with the earth embroidered on the front in the shape of a bright butterfly. It was there. I spun around, everything sparkling, every cell of me shouting yes, and went back for more.

MORE THAN I KNEW HOW TO ASK

I REMEMBER THE WARM JULY MORNING when I first walked into my office at Third Presbyterian Church in Rochester, New York, to begin my first "real job" as a minister. The room was beautiful with its high white ceiling, deep blue carpet, and tall window overlooking the trees on the street below. There was a bouquet of flowers, sent by my parents. There was also a pile of file folders, each full of committee minutes, sent by the senior pastor, Gene Bay. Where in the world to start? I sat down at the desk, took out the pad of paper I had brought, and a pen. I began to write. I wrote about how overwhelmed I felt, and how excited. It was a big, historic, activist metropolitan church.

I got up, opened the window, and sat down to write some more. Toward the bottom of the page, my writing turned to prayer, and I felt God embrace me in my desire to love well. I could not know yet all the people who would walk in the door of that office, what questions and stories they would bring, or what enlivening gifts. I could not begin to imagine the courage their courage would call forth in me, or the openings we would create together into spiritual vibrancy, racial justice, and shared economic well-being. I had no inkling that we would learn and risk our way into taking a stand for the ordination of lesbian, gay, bisexual, and transgendered members of our denomination—or that during this process, the truth of my lesbian orientation would come clear to me.

But one late afternoon, getting up from my desk to stretch and look outside, I saw

Michal crossing the street from the church to the parking lot. She was wearing tight jeans and western boots, swinging her long legs and a silver-gray briefcase, tossing her silver-gray hair. I'd heard she'd been hired to help a struggling city church, New Life Presbyterian, figure out whether to close. That church is thriving now, with Stewart and Mary Jo Pattison as co-pastors. After Michal and I fell in love, and after MJ and Stewart came to Rochester, we four became friends. But that was later. The day I looked out my window and saw Michal walking, it was just Wow. Ahh. Ooh.

EXILE

TURNING A PAGE IN THIS MORNING'S *Arizona Daily Star* I was caught undefended by a headline declaring the Presbyterian Church's latest vote to exile me. Across our living room, Michal read a novel, the sun bright on her hair. I keep asking, "How did this happen? How did I get here?" When I went with my friends to Elmhurst Presbyterian, I found a love that has never stopped growing, and this has turned out to be a problem between the church and me. I believed it when they said that love does not come intact and finished, but is new every morning, deeper every evening, an ongoing, lifelong work. Now the church says I am evil for loving God like this—with ever more of my heart, mind, soul, and body. Now they call it a sin that I have grown to love the world with this much tenderness and power.

WHEREVER LOVE MAY LEAD

THE SUN HAS JUST FLOODED THIS DESK where I am drinking a cup of licorice tea. I am lonely this morning in the world. Sometimes it feels as if I have gone into a different place from where other people live. This is terrifying for one who was taught from the crib to make it clear at every turn that I fit in. And yet the seeds of my growing beyond this were planted long ago— in church. There in the sanctuary at Elmhurst Presbyterian I heard the preachers say, not just once, but many times, from many vista points in the terrain of our faith, that we are not here to conform to the ways of this world, but to be renewed by the inner transformation of our hearts and minds. *That was it!* I got a whole new way to make sense of—and to dedicate—my life.

In those days I did not imagine that my yes to this call would lead me to be rejected by the church. But now, in my strength, in my love, I know the national church's delegates are wrong when they keep voting that my life is "not God's wish." Their decision makes me wonder what else the church is mistaken about, and what other kinds of harm their ways of believing do.

For now, by ardent faith, I seek to write a way through the church's oppression to wherever love may lead. In faith, I recognize and affirm myself for this. This is part of my trusting God, this courageous knowing and freeing of my self to move about, breathing and becoming, even in this world as it is.

TWO TREASURES

THIS MORNING IN BENTLEY'S CAFÉ, TILLY told me stories of growing up in Georgia, singing hymns and hearing sermons at the Presbyterian church, and how she draws on that inspiration now as she teaches and writes. I muddled around, trying to utter the devastation I feel when people invoke our tradition in a way that despises my life—and then cover the tracks of their interpretive work by saying God's word "makes" them condemn me. Listening intently through the steam that rose from our coffee, Tilly took a sip from her cup and asked, "Aren't we the words of God?"

Later as we were leaving she turned back to the baskets of pastries. "How about something for Michal? What does she like?" Tilly bought one and handed the white paper bag to me. I walked home smiling, swinging two treasures, Tilly's faith, so healing and emboldening, and a cranberry orange scone, Michal's favorite.

BEREFT OF WORDS

MOST TIMES I AM QUIET IN A GROUP FOR awhile, listening, and gradually it comes clear what I want to say. One night at Third Church, though, I dearly desired to find words, to speak of the ground on which I stood, but could not figure out even how to hint at it, gesture toward it, invoke it with so much as a whisper.

We were under siege. Ministers from three other Presbyterian churches in Rochester were about to bring charges against us for our openness to people of all sexual identities. They came to our church that night to talk us into revoking our statement of welcome. They stood, one by one, and made their case. The last minister argued hotly that we had violated "the teachings of the church." This phrase bewildered me, since I had never before heard it in Presbyterian conversation, but as he repeated it, I started to wonder whether our stance *should* be thrown out. Despite my heart's trust in our work, despite the evidence of my life, and regardless of my strong solidarity with the other gay people and our allies in the room, I began to feel that he was right, and I was wrong.

It was hard to breathe. I could think of no argument against him. I did not yet know how to do any of the things I wanted to—stand up for the sacredness of my life, defend the wonderful work of congregational members, gay and straight, or voice an alternative view of how to interpret our denomination's traditions. I sat in a horrified and paralyzed silence.

The anguish of my silence stayed with me. Over the years, with steady purpose, I let it lead me to enter an extensive research into the workings of religious authority and interpretation. I still wish I had been able to speak up that night, even if it had been only to shout, "Hey, you're talking about *our lives!*" But I said nothing of the sort. I said not a single word. I wasn't even free to say "our lives" in public yet, because though by that time I did know myself as lesbian, I didn't want to be a court case, or split our congregation—I wanted to be a pastor, that was all.

DOING DISHES

MORNING. I JUST FINISHED DOING DISHES again. Again, as light comes to the leaves of the trees framed by this window. Again, as the birds come into the yard for water. My soul, too, needs to do things over and over. Like feel its anger, trace the textures, consider the counsel, ride the unruly surf. A cup slips out of my sudsy fingers. It cracks and splinters. I shout and soar.

At home and school and church, as I grew, many voices urged me not to have any anger. Even feeling frustrated came to seem like doing something wrong. It has taken me so long to untangle myself from these teachings that I hesitate to acknowledge, even to myself, that I am only now beginning to be able to notice when I am angry. It is embarrassing to admit that I have actually seen anger as something not allowed for me—because I was trained to be pleasing, because I am a woman, because I am a minister, because I have dedicated myself to love.

My feelings of anger, I now see, have often been elbowed aside by fear—fear of rejection, of retaliation, of being different in yet another way. My surges of anger, even at actions that harm me, are also sometimes crushed, before I notice, by guilt. It is as if I am not supposed to care that I am being wronged. Yet the more I continue to explore my anger, the more I cease to blame myself for being injured by the violence of oppression. Instead, I begin to imagine, and live in, a very different world. I realize that oppressors are capable of change. I hold them accountable to join in creating freedom and well-being for us all.

I pray to the Breath of Life... be with all

of us who enter this liberation struggle, rise in us with our anger, and spark in us a love courageous enough to bring a gift of healing to our world. Visit us in ordinary hours. Help us to notice when all is not well. Renew our trust that we need not go someplace else, or do something else, or be someone else in order to claim our liberation. Thanks be to you for the occasion of here and now.

BE IT RESOLVED

THE PHONE RANG EXTRA EARLY THAT morning. It was Josefina saying that her blessing of union with Helen would not be allowed to take place in the sanctuary of their church. This was the Presbyterian congregation where Michal and I belonged for our first few years in Tucson, before we found a more wholehearted welcome at St. Mark's.

The governing board was divided and could not resolve to open the sanctuary for this ceremony. Josefina was a member of that board, elected and ordained to spiritual leadership by the congregation. A few months before, that same board had adopted a Statement of Inclusive Faith. "Be it resolved," the Statement concluded, following a blaze of prophetic theologizing and a spirited account of the congregation's years of solidarity with oppressed peoples: "Be it resolved that this congregation declares its welcome to all persons seeking to follow Christ into the full life, ministry, and leadership of its community of faith, regardless of race, ethnicity, worldly condition, gender, disability, or sexual orientation."

What happened?

Fear took hold.

When the board circulated its Statement in meetings among church members, most voiced their strong support, but several objected to the mention of sexual orientation. As the controversy grew, some members called for more study of "the issue." One proposed adopting only the theology and history parts of the Statement, thus avoiding any "Be it resolved." Eventually board members decided not to take their usual next step of putting the Statement to a congregational vote. But they insisted that they stood behind their Statement of Inclusive Faith one hundred percent. Until they shut the door on Fina and Helen.

What *happened*?

Oh fear. That's right. I forgot. I lost sight for a moment of the threat that Helen and Fina posed. Two women. Two races. Two healers in our community who wanted to go to their church and make their vows.

As soon as we hung up, I felt the rebuke. It landed like a kick in the gut.

Right away I went rotten, saw myself as walking garbage, turned into the abomination they kept saying we were. I recoiled from my own body as if it would poison sacred spaces. I felt the horror of believing that my being would bring harm.

Lock the sanctuary. Fence the table. Don't let the blessing of Helen and Fina's communion be accomplished on your holy ground.

I ranted. I cried. I walked. I prayed.

My breath returned. My vision cleared. I still miss the people of that congregation, their faces around the table, our voices together softly in prayer. But their pretense broke the slender, necessary strands of human trust. Their purge gave the nod to further violence against queer people. Their decision to sacrifice us in obedience to their fears was an abomination.

This morning, as my body remembers the hurt of their betrayals, be it resolved that, once again, I will shake the dust off these two beautiful feet and take this joyous, radiant dance of mine on down the road.

I REPENT

THEY CALL ME AN UNREPENTANT homosexual. But they don't know me well. To repent is "to turn." What I do is keep turning toward this love in my heart. And this leads me to a turning away from hatred.

I repent. I repent of swallowing hatred's lies. I repent of assenting to hatred's threats. I repent of adjusting to the everyday habits of hatred.

I repent. I repent of excusing hatred's ways. I repent of being silenced by hatred's snares. I repent of seeking a home within the world according to hatred.

I repent. I repent. I repent. I repent. I repent. Thanks be to God for this rising from the dead.

How You Call to Me, Jesus

SOFTLY AND TENDERLY IS HOW YOU CALL
to me, Jesus, and reverently, playfully, too.
In daylight and darkness. Come trouble or
pleasure. I listen, and find myself beloved.
I tell my truth, and find myself believed.

MONSOON

WHEN MICHAL, MARY CAROL, AND I SAT out in the desert this evening, our hair wet, our bodies glad for the sudden heat from the rocks beneath us, I was tasting resurrection. I welcome it whenever I can, with a wafting of yeast when we baked yesterday, a shimmer of lightning in the belly of a cloud—with the rain cool on our faces as we watched the layered mountains to the west turn the color of watermelon, then violets.

No one said a word. Except about the delicious earth, the bats tilting by. The greening of ocotillo since the monsoon finally arrived. This was prayer for us. We met in our attraction to the holy. We just sat there opening to the Sacred... her undaunted generosity, her irrepressible skill.

On our way back, the truck hummed and mumbled through the pass. "Oh!"—a huge moon, golden, liquid, took us by surprise. We sang. MC told a story. We laughed so hard it took all three of us to drive.

ONE VOICE

I WONDER IF PEGGY WAY HAS ANY IDEA how much she has blessed my life, helping me say yes through all these years, as much as I could at every turn, to who I really am. At seminary, she was the only one talking about the variety of human sexualities as an expression of the divine. Right there in her 1979 Vanderbilt Divinity School classroom, she said so. And wrote about it, published it, too. Sometimes it only takes one voice to provide enough shelter to help us take the risk of becoming ourselves. Peggy gave me this gift, and I still have it. May we all come to trust the abundance of freedom that can be set in motion when we speak.

Whosoever May

EVERYBODY CAME TO MY GRANDPARENTS' house by stepping from the side porch into the kitchen. A bright, warm room with a floor of brick-red linoleum, its walls were taken up with large windows, a broad stove, white wood cupboards, a tall refrigerator, a sink with its drainer full of clean dishes, and a counter topped with a thermos of hot coffee, a bread box stocked with doughnuts, and the clutter of my grandmother Jessie's artwork—jars, brushes, oils, chalks, pencils, sketches, and paintings in various stages of creation. Somehow, there was room in the middle of all this for a long maple table and plenty of chairs.

As far back as I can remember, that table was covered with a red and white checked cloth, and my grandmother always set an extra place for supper. When I asked why, she said it was "for Whosoever May." At first I thought that was somebody's name, maybe somebody from the South. But after awhile I came to understand that she set that place for "whosoever may appear." And sure enough, people did. Neighbors stopped by. Relatives came over. Young people without a safe home found a place. And during my grandparents' last few years, each fall when the leaves turned, I would take a week off and drive a northern route above the Great Lakes from New York or Wisconsin to Cadillac, Michigan.

I remember waking to the aroma of cinnamon toast baking in my grandmother's oven. Coming down the steep stairs in the early morning dark, I'd find her in the living room, just one lamp on over her corner chair, her fingers tracing slowly down the page of a book or curled around a pen as she kept her journal. In her eighties she joined the first crop of people writing letters on email, took a course in metaphysics, tuned her short-wave radio to news of the world, and welcomed Michal into her heart.

On the morning after we buried my grandfather, I sat beside Grandmother Jessie in the back pew of her Christian Science church. Red leaves blew from the maple tree outside the windows. She got up and turned the heater on. While the woman lector read, we dozed, sinking into a strange, delicious rest that still reaches across these years to console me. A hymn woke us, and we stood. Her voice came out soft, high, and clear.

Just before Thanksgiving that year, my grandmother also passed on. She died the way she wanted to, resting in comfort at the Grander View Christian Science Care Center. She did research, reserved a room, and hired an ambulance for $300 to drive her downstate. Only after she settled in did she phone her children to tell them where she was. On her last morning, she ate breakfast in bed and drifted away not long after, with sun shining in through the window and an attendant reading to her from Mary Baker Eddy.

The last time I saw her was the windy, wet Monday after my grandfather died. My dad and I had stayed with her for an extra night and awakened to a thunderstorm. We three drank coffee and ate doughnuts in the kitchen like so many times before. Then Dad and I got ready to drive back to Chicago in time for my plane back to Tucson. We hauled suitcases and fancy-clothes bags down from upstairs. We ran in and out, packing the car. My grandmother sat at that table of hers, watching us with impish blue eyes. I think she knew. I suspected nothing. She smiled. I kissed her and ran out into the rain.

Too Wonderful

AS I LISTEN IN CHURCHES FOR WHAT IS said about love, I am troubled by how rarely we are encouraged to love ourselves. Practically all the sermons and hymns and rituals conspire to deter us from it. What for? Why such avid prohibition, especially since Jesus spoke of loving ourselves in the same breath with loving God and loving each other as the deepest calling of our lives? Maybe it's that loving ourselves is so disruptive to our hopelessness. Maybe loving ourselves leads to "too much" faith, "too many" glimpses of how very different our life together could be—so brave, so just, so thrilling, so joyous that from where we stand now it really does seem too wonderful to believe.

It Could Be Otherwise

THE AIR IS DIFFERENT THIS MORNING, fresh in my hair, cool through my body as I breathe and sigh and hear the voices of birds coming into our neighborhood again, some to stay for winter, some to rest in the willows and mesquites before they fly many more miles south. I am different, too. I have grown out of dismissing my hopes the way I used to, out of adjusting to the insults of liturgies, out of pretending that the crumbs I brushed together under patriarchy's table could be turned into a loaf. I know now that it could be otherwise—the church, I mean; my life is already changed.

WHOEVER IS READY

TONIGHT AS THE LIGHT BEGINS TO FADE I want to sit on the back porch of my childhood house, look at shadows on the grass, and eat a peach with my mother, the juice dripping down our chins. Not that I don't have a peach here. But I want to feel at home.

I call to Maggie. Out on the patio, I brush her hair, the shiny black, the wispy white, the streaks and speckles of brown. I toss her ball and she takes off after it, a twelve-year-old collie breaking into a puppy's delirious run.

On the news, violence is told as if nothing else can be imagined. My heart can no longer listen as if there were no other way.

May I learn to see every body, none left out, as bone, like my bone, of sacred bone; and flesh, like my flesh, of love, God's own. May I learn this with others. When the way is difficult, may our vision carry us. When the way is impossible, may our desire carry us.

May whoever is ready, or almost ready, go first.

I Am Here

I WAKE UP WITH LIGHT JUST BEGINNING to visit our bedroom. Power is running through my limbs, from my head and heart out into my fingers and toes. I am vibrating. Who knows what will happen today? I am here. I listen to bird songs, watch mesquite branches dance on the wind, and welcome this trust that opens a space for the work and play of my being with God. Who knows what will happen today? I am vibrating. I am here.

TALL GRASS

THE GRASS IS OVER MY HEAD. OVER AND over, my head needs to rest in a nest of grass leaning back into the late afternoon of childhood where I can smell the apples on the wind. Apples, they say, are sin, but I say, what could be sweeter?

HANGING LAUNDRY

ONLY IN RECENT YEARS HAVE I KNOWN that my denomination has a maxim on its seal, "Reformed—Always Reforming." Reaching up to hang clean socks on the line this afternoon, glimpsing the red brick buildings of the university over our weathered fence, I realized that my becoming a scholar in rhetoric arose partly because I wanted to figure out how to extricate myself from the oppressions of the church while treasuring its gifts, how to lift my voice in the controversies, going back to Jesus and before, over what are faithful, loving interpretations of my spiritual tradition. I dropped a clothespin on the ground, picked it up and brushed the red-brown dirt off on my jeans, then hung the second corner of a

58

pillowcase. That's what Christian faith is, I thought, with all its rituals and texts, including the scriptures—an always still unfolding conversation about how to make sense of Jesus, God, love, and our own lives.

ALL HERE

YET AGAIN THIS MORNING, I HAVE wrestled with temptations to forsake parts of me that meet with hostility in the world, and I have made another decision to be all here. I am learning to love my particular self, rather than trying so hard to be some other.

When African American Pentecostal preacher James Forbes was Visiting Theologian for a conference on racial justice at Third Church, we celebrated communion at Sunday morning worship. I stood beside him at the broad table in that beautiful, old sanctuary with rafters high above and the smell of wood all around. People were gathered into the curved pews that circled the table and spread outward in every direction toward stained glass windows and doors. I glanced over as James was about to give the invitation, expecting him to say the traditional opening words, "This is the joyful feast of the people of God." Instead, what he spoke was a question, gentle and arresting as it floated out over us and hung in the air: "Is everybody here?"

For a moment I took his question practically, as if he were asking if all six hundred or so of us were in the room. I nearly dashed out to check the hallway for teenagers playing hooky. But just in time, I began to be more profoundly moved. Maybe James meant to challenge us, to point out how almost everyone there was affluent and white. Maybe he was inviting us to taste bread with some who were not literally in the room because of hierarchies of race and class. Maybe he wanted to spark our receptivity to the spiritual presence of Jesus, along with other loved ones who have died.

From here, I also think James maybe wanted to ask if we were willing to be truly present at that table, for that moment, in our own souls and bodies. Were we ready to be known to ourselves and to each other and to God as we opened our mouths to taste this communion? James' voice, which came rumbling and crackling like a thunderstorm when he preached, was so vulnerable when he came to the table and made his question. Now more than ever, I understand why— such was the love he was asking us to summon. Is everybody here?

EASY AS BREATHING

SPIRIT OF LIFE, WE ARE EVER AND always protected, for you are with us. Over and over, you prepare before us tables where we can taste and see that there really is more than enough to go around. More than enough food, yes. And more than enough power. Our part is to notice, take pleasure, believe. Here on this cool grass beside the stream I rest in you and the impossible turns out to be effortless. I watch a green-blue lizard jump; I listen to the locusts keen. With such gentleness, I steal away. Easy as breathing, I go free.

PART OF THE GIFT

TONIGHT I AM WRITING BESIDE OUR fireplace where I can watch orange flames flow upward into the dark. There is something deeply comforting to me about the dark. When I first heard the gospel story of how Nicodemus went by night to talk with Jesus, I could hardly believe my ears. I remembered immediately my going after dark to St. Mary's Church in Nashville to visit Gilbert D'Souza.

I would drive downtown, park in the church lot, and come to a side door where Gilbert would meet me. It was mostly dark inside, too, with the deep red glow of candles burning in the hallways. Our footsteps echoed on the tiled steps. We rarely saw anyone else. In a small warm room, we sat and talked. I kept saying there must be something I should do to make sure I didn't miss God's grace in my life. Gilbert, my chosen spiritual advisor, also my exegesis teacher and a Jesuit priest from India, did not think so. He was always surprising me, and still does to this day.

Stephanie, another divinity student, and I used to invite him to our apartment for festive meals. The first time we opened the door and saw him standing there holding his briefcase, we teased him. "Don't you ever stop working? Were you reading theology on the bus?" Gilbert smiled. He came in and sat down on our old green sofa, set his case flat across his knees and snapped open the cover. We all burst out laughing when he pulled out a bottle of wine, Blue Nun, chilled and ready to drink.

One Sunday I visited a service at St. Mary's. From the pulpit, Gilbert's dark face shone, serious and intent, while his words floated among us in the gentlest preaching voice I have ever heard. During our conversations, too, Gilbert spoke softly. He told me he sometimes prayed upside down, doing yoga. He told me I was "a natural" at exegesis. Best of all, he told me, in a whisper and with utter assurance, "You don't have to go around unbuttoned to grace. It just shows up, this love we scarcely know how to yearn for, and part of the gift is, we notice."

OUT OF OUR SHOES

NINETEEN YEARS AGO, WHEN MICHAL AND I had our ceremony, we hid it from nearly everyone we knew. We held it at one of the Presbyterian churches in Rochester where a lesbian was pastor. We scheduled it for six-thirty in the morning on a weekday so no one would be found out. Gathered around us in the old wooden chancel were nine very dedicated friends and our wonderful son Thomas, a teenager then. Most of us showed up with hair still wet from the shower. Just as we were about to begin, a vacuum cleaner started up with a roar, and the pastor ran down the hall to ask the church custodian to take a break for a little while.

Our friend Barbara Jones-Hagedorn, the minister for our celebration, preached us out of our shoes. Telling the love of Ruth and Naomi, she swept us up, whirled us into the mystery of divine presence, then set us down again in the place where we had begun, but new, transfigured, never to be the same. Later she told us she had looked up from her book during the blessing prayers and seen the hair of our bowed heads—mine brown, and Michal's silver—intermingling. I remember Barbara's voice sounding into my soul with those prayers, and the passion in how she spoke the words "defend them from every enemy." I remember the joined voices of our loved ones, too, as they made a vow to stand by us, and the embraces we shared around the circle when all the words were done.

Next we all went down the street for breakfast at the home of two of the attenders. Sun streamed through the dining room windows onto a table filled with fruit and bread and eggs and coffee and champagne and flowers. We feasted and told stories. We laughed and took pictures. Then we two drove off in our sky blue VW Rabbit for a honey-moon of hiking in the early springtime hills and woods and streams of upstate New York.

SITTING WITH SAINT FRANCIS

LIKE JESUS, I LOVE TO PRAY IN LONELY places. One is the rickety redwood chair in a far corner of our yard, under a mesquite tree and between two creosote bushes that bloom yellow in the spring and attract bees that hum. Saint Francis is back there, too. He arrived several years ago on a bright cool afternoon just before Christmas. Michal's parents drove over and rang our bell. When we came out, they lifted him from the trunk of their car. In meandering procession, we carried him around the yard and finally planted him in that shady alcove. I go out almost every day, shake mesquite leaves from the chair cushion, and sit beside him. From there I have seen a willow tree grow tall and an oak get so thick with shiny leaves that grackles, sparrows, mockingbirds, and woodpeckers can all hide at once in its branches. Watching these trees extend their beauty has helped me to grow into my own. I also watch ants, clouds, and butterflies. Sometimes I tell Saint Francis about my struggles. The bird on his head seems to ease my shyness. I smile and stroke his cheek with my fingers, honoring him, honoring Michal's mother, who has also passed on now, and somehow, in the generous interplay of spirits, honoring me.

Making Soup

THIS MORNING I AM AT THE EPIC CAFÉ ON Fourth Avenue. At another table a woman is balancing her rumpled checkbook while eating a cinnamon roll with nuts on top, drinking coffee, and watching the sun come up over the church across the street. It is a Presbyterian church in need of a pastor. I look at the doors of the church and then at myself, over here, across the street, ruled out, writing in this café instead of in a pastor's office. Behind the counter a woman is making a pie, crimping the edges of the bottom crust with the butt of a knife, wearing a white apron turned down and tied around her waist. Now Elvis is singing that he's all shook up and yes, so am I, and I am also seeking balance, wondering if the costs of becoming myself will be overtaken by the blessings someday. I find comfort in knowing that I am wholeheartedly in the struggle for freedom now. The woman who was crimping the pie crust is now frying onions in butter, probably for today's soup. The aroma is rich and delicious. At lunch time people will eat her soup and it will strengthen them to go on tending friendships, drafting poems, fixing bicycles, loving children, growing organic tomatoes, and doing other wonderful things that we often do not hear about in the news. This writing I do is perhaps not so different from making soup. I sauté the ingredients of my soul's yearning, add courage, and simmer them into what I hope will be a nourishing meal for people who want to become more freely and joyously who they are.

SNOW DAYS

TODAY I MISS BEING PASTOR WITH THE people at First Presbyterian Church in Green Bay, where I was called after my ministry in Rochester. Often snow would be falling past our church windows while inside we were singing, praying, eating, sharing our lives. I left there hoping I could go back someday and be forthcoming about who I am. When the time was right, last spring, I went. It felt wonderful to see everybody and to step outside our former silences, but also sad because I knew more clearly than ever the extent of what we had lost. My hiding, which had allowed our journey, had also compromised my friendship with everyone in the church. It had diminished our capacity to bless each other and the world.

But more than ever, too, I am happy for our miracle: though we were caught in a web of oppressions, we found ways to love each other well.

AMARYLLIS

A LOPSIDED OVAL MOON WAS BRIGHT IN the East this morning when Michal and I looked out from our living room window, over the leaves of the amaryllis plant we bought at the drugstore last week. When we opened the box, we saw that it had already sent up a long stalk that crumpled when it ran into the cardboard top. It seemed to have decided to grow no matter what. The stalk has turned from white to yellow to deep green in the sun over these past few days. It now stands tall with five pink and white blooms emerging. How beautiful, and what a lesson for me on how to live by faith, how to begin coming forth without knowing ahead of time whether a habitable space will open.

My mother remembers that in her womb, I often pushed and stretched as if to say, "there's not enough room for me in here." Sometimes I feel that way now, too. In the feminist theology course I taught last fall, I mentioned my sense that the world is far from ready for who I am and what I want to say. Julie Jung looked back at me with her amazing smile. "Some of us are ready," she said.

CHRISTMAS HINT

ON THIS CHRISTMAS EVE, I WONDER IF Jesus might grieve that we focus so exclusively on his entry into this world that we miss the miracle of our own. I am beginning to think he would rejoice if we started to look upon our births—and rebirths—as being just as full of divine possibilities as his was.

I marvel at the survival of the two gospel stories that tell how Jesus rejected a woman because she belonged to a different race and culture from himself, but then turned around and helped her, in response to her wisdom and power. Jesus listened. Jesus repented. There in the midst of his teaching and healing, Jesus embraced the spiritual growing he needed to do. Rather than cling to his old way of seeing, Jesus made a leap of faith. Instead of pretending to be perfect, Jesus decided to love.

On this Christmas Eve, I wonder... What if incarnation turned out to be not perfect and not scarce? What if the divine-human love unfolding in Jesus was not a one-time-only event but a marvelous hint, a wondrous clue to what could happen, what already sometimes takes place, in our being with each other, with the world, with ourselves? What if Christmas were a time when we learned together how to recognize—how to become—God with us?

LET THERE BE A JOY

THESE DAYS WHEN I AM TEMPTED TO HIDE and silence myself again, desperate for relief from the penalties and threats of oppression, I remember the community of courageous people taking one step, then the next, into liberating love, in spaces both personal and public, all over the world. This stretch of my journey is wrenching, and how could it be otherwise, when I am rolling away the stone that had contained such deep losses, fears, and indignations, and so steadily entering into my rising from the dead? I give thanks this night, Sacred Spirit, for every time somebody rises up to tell her truth and in that act opens up more room for each of us to tell our own. Bless our ruminations. Be heard in the many resonances of our talk. Be recognized upon our faces as we eat and listen and hurt and laugh and touch and remember and dream. May we have reverence for the borders between our selves and each other, a reverence that refrains from making assumptions and dares to welcome the mystery of whatever may be going on inside another person's skin. More and more, especially in the turbulent times of our struggle, show us that we are not abandoned. And in our finding you right here with us, let there be a joy.

At My Stove or Desk

YOU VISIT SO UNOBTRUSIVELY. USUALLY at my stove or desk. I sense you looking over my shoulder with interest in whatever I am making: a letter to Deborah, a retreat for women pastors, a minestrone soup, a feminist practice of faith. When you come, I am surprised at first, but then it's, "Of course! What did I expect?"

There are many things I don't know about how life was for you. Much was hidden, as much was given, in your ways of finding strength. Grandmother, I am inspired by you: your intellectual pursuits, your mysticism, your curiosity, your artistry, your hospitality, your stubbornness, your joy. You were willing to learn and willful in being yourself—a courageous blend which continues to offer wisdom for liberation.

Grandmother, I call on your assistance. I open to your power. Be with me, help me to trust my life in these days as I sink into my heart and proceed to invent pleasures and blessings of my own.

REAL LOVE

I BELIEVE MORE THAN EVER THAT, IN keeping with real love, God wants to hear our real voices. If this were not true, God would be like our oppressors. "He"—or "She"—would be a jealous God who lords it over us, who is afraid of women's self-determination, who worries that our wisdoms do not heal, but bring harm. Such a God would want us to find in our hearts only compliance. But the healing heart is a wild, untidy, fluid, surprising region. It embraces light, shadow, darkness, colors, contradictions, seeming impossibilities. If we turn to our hearts and listen, we will often hear a jumble of voices. The borders are often blurry between our resignation and our tenacity, our terror and boldness, our guilt and anger, our love and our shame. If we are willing, we can learn to hear the struggle between our internalized oppressions and our emerging valiant, wondrous, loving, irreplaceable selves.

Listening with such reverence to my heart, I see more clearly than ever that to enter divine presence is not to submit, but to fall in love. To help me know this, I sometimes speak of God as Sophia, Divine Wisdom. I thank her for her very present help in flowers and food and friends. I thank her for her boundless, buoyant trust in our capacity to love. Sophia has no rod or staff to keep us subdued and "safe." Her softening eyes, her listening voice, her warm embrace, her breathtaking smile— these are the gifts with which she meets us in our struggles. She even seems to agree with the apostle Paul when he wrote that "love does not insist on its own way"—and I say, not even divine love! least of all divine love!—which has so steadfastly attracted and encouraged and sparked and cheered us out from under domination.

$\mathbb{C}$
SEE WHAT HAPPENS

MAGGIE CAME AND GAVE MY WRIST A WET nudge this morning so I wouldn't forget our walk. She pranced through our neighborhood, thoroughly thrilled, and I took long strides to keep up. At the corner of 10th and Mountain the folks with the lavender swing on their porch had been out watering. The daisies burst forth with burnt red from gangly stems; the gazanias were still asleep. The sun fell warm on my cheek. I inhaled the wet desert. Music splurged out the screen door, electric piano and drums, jubilant, and I whispered a prayer of thanks.

See what happens when a Presbyterian minister trusts the love she learned in church? It's quite a discipline. I get up early. I write, eat toast and raspberries, go walking with Maggie. I have a bubble bath, write, take a nap, make up a new recipe. Michal and I eat out back under the pomegranate trees. We hear the hummingbird zip by, feel the stirrings of coolness, talk until our voices float between us in the dark.

Discipline, our friend Deborah Mullen announces via a note on her refrigerator, is the art of remembering what you want. We talked today about our denomination's fear of members who pray to Sophia, even though it's a biblically rooted way to invoke divine presence. Deborah, a womanist theologian, pointed out that liberation becomes more possible as the suppression of women's power in our churches becomes more overt. Daunting as it is to see the church's hostility toward us so clearly, we can use this opportunity to deepen our understanding of the challenges we face.

But who can keep a sidewalk from

becoming holy ground? I walk along, and there you are... Sophia. Who can prevent this joy of recognition, these rejuvenations of faith? Sophia God. Sophia Jesus. Sophia Spirit. The more I say your name, the more I see you.

SOPHIA OF THE SPLENDID GRASS

THIS AFTERNOON ONLY A FEW SOULS, drawn to our solitude, walked the hard-packed sand along the water. I heard waves rolling slowly in, but could not see them. A soft, velvet fog lay upon the dunes, then receded, like a curtain slowly presenting the vast magnificence of Lake Michigan, and then floated back in, enfolding me again. I sat down on the sand, leaned against a long, gray driftwood tree, and went with my tears.

Camp Saugatuck was my adolescent self's most sacred landscape, a place I journeyed to over many years for winter retreats and summer camps, a place of mystery and beauty, of intimacy and play, where I awakened ever more deeply to divine presence as my church took me into its arms and sang to me of love.

But today, years later, grown up, there on that same beach, I let myself feel the assault of their betrayal: "The love we proclaimed could never have called forth *you*."

Now more than ever, my love for my life, for Jesus, and for the world is growing deeper. I pray to one who is not afraid for me to grow. Sophia. Sophia of the fragrant pines, Sophia of the splendid grass, Sophia of the rolling waves, I look back through all the seasons of my life and recognize you. You this whole way. You in the times of joy and challenge. Your invitation, your embrace, your song, your promise. I am doing it! I am loving. And here you are again—loving me.

BESIDE THE STREAM

THIS MORNING AS MICHAL AND I walked beside a stream below the Baboquivari Mountains we saw the startling first green on towering cottonwoods. I could feel my soul leafing out, too. A gentle rain had fallen as the sunlight warmed us, and afterward everything was shining—the wide blue sky, the floating white clouds, the silver-brown rock, the black phoebe tipping to drink from a branch above the water. I could feel my soul tipping, too.

WHAT JESUS WROTE

I PLUNGE IN HERE TODAY WITHOUT knowing quite how, and not demanding some sort of finished performance, but just to open a place in which to find what I want to say.

I believe Jesus understands my need to open space this way. The gospels say that he was one for whom there was no room even to be born, one who came to his own people and "they received him not," one whose body was shattered, whose voice and breath were stolen on a cross put up by the oppressors of his day. They killed him so they could go on refusing to risk a deeper courage. They silenced him as an announcement to others that there was no room in their world for such an untamed love.

I hope that the oppressors of my day don't decide there is no room in their world for my voice, my love, my breath, my body. Some days I wish I fit in better with what the oppressors want to hear and know. When I wish that, I feel it as an insult to who I actually am and what I deeply desire. When I wish that, I see the depth of my fear of harm from others, for I am also aware of the radical love I have for my own miraculous, imperfect, unfolding humanity, and for our world, and I know that I do not really want to hide. I want to be seen and heard. I want to be known.

Jesus was bold in his willingness to be here, speaking his startling truths and loving people who weren't seen as worthy of love, like that time the oppressors brought him a woman they called a sinner and expected to be able to stone her to death. They brought her as a test for him. What he did was write. Jesus bent down and wrote in the dust with his finger and no one knows anymore what he wrote but my faith is that he was making room, first within his own heart and then in the predicament they had set, for a wild and healing love to enter, room for a woman to survive the afternoon, room for himself also to keep breathing and walking and dreaming for at least another day. I love Jesus for wanting all that, for risking it, too, and for staying with me, still wild, still healing, still rising from the dead, as I take my turn of being here: seen, heard, known as who I am who I am who I am who I am who I am.

FOOLISHNESS INVOLVED

THERE IS A CERTAIN FOOLISHNESS involved in my willingness to love Jesus, or anyone else, including myself. When I love, I open myself to the hurt that goes with change, with loss, with sharing in someone's struggle. It seems strange all of a sudden that in loving Jesus, I have all along been loving someone who has already in some sense been lost to me, someone whose voice I never got to hear, someone I never got to share food with, or laughter, or tears. I realize tonight that Jesus is the first person I knew who had already died before I loved him.

Extra Much Sweetness

HERE I AM AGAIN, SHOWING UP TO write. It is one of my ways of rising to the challenge of loving my life as I make my way through a world that is in so many ways hostile toward me. Again and again, the act of writing releases me from bitterness and resignation. I am so thankful for this, for life is wonderfully sweet, I know. One of my spiritual practices is to make sure I taste this sweetness extra much. So I'll go out into the back yard now, and smell the springtime desert earth, and open my soul to divinity writing letters to me everywhere in the bright new leaves of this glorious morning.

I LOVE JESUS WALKING

I LOVE JESUS WALKING OUT AMONG THE Galilean desert hills alone. I love Jesus eating and talking and laughing and hoping with friends. I love Jesus weeping over Jerusalem because its people could not love. I love Jesus living as if there is plenty—of power, money, honor, pleasure, bread. I love Jesus meeting up with divine presence in the everyday chores, errands, and conversations of a life. I love Jesus believing the word of a woman who argued that he had some spiritual growing to do. I love Jesus figuring out how to love even when harassed by people who were capitulating to hatred. I love Jesus rereading and transforming the traditions of his Jewish spiritual life. I love Jesus making room for me by the playfulness of his teaching. I love Jesus alerting me that what the church says about love, about God, about me, about what is possible, may not be worthy of my trust. I love Jesus showing me how to live in creative resistance to the despair that prevails around us. I love Jesus inspiring me to slip outside the momentum of oppression, to steal away to a place where I am not entirely possessed, a place where I am able to remember my dissents and dreams and powers. I love Jesus who comes to me in times of trial, who lifts the burden of the world's contempt by witnessing to my infinite worth, who is here now, in the midst of my fears, to guard my dignity, to help me keep on writing.

I WANT COMMUNION

I DON'T BELIEVE DIVINE LOVE IS ANY more available to us after the killing of Jesus than before it, when he was alive, trusting in it, pointing to it, participating in its power. I don't believe we "have to" let the evil of that torture and murder take over again (as if it were God's idea of help) each time we share a holy meal. I want communion to be about abundance: a feast of multiplying gifts, kinships, possibilities, hopes, loaves, pleasures—a time to practice living as if divinity showers humanity with more than enough to go around.

A Call to Life

MY CALLING IS TO ACT WITH COURAGE IN the direction of justice, but I would not be somehow more faithful if I were harmed along the way. I want to thrive! I believe human beings have the power to forsake violence—that *this* is how well-being emerges. It is good to return home in the evening and enjoy one's supper, then go forth the next morning to love the world for another day.

EYES WIDE OPEN

BESIDE OUR FRONT DOORSTEP, A DESERT verbena has planted itself and bloomed bright purple. It reminds me of how I hope. In order to survive, my hope sends roots down underneath our usual assumptions about what is possible in our common life. In such hope, I look with eyes wide open at the momentum of violence in our world and yet do not allow my deepest desires to be muted, ruined, starved for breath and nourishment. Sometimes called unrealistic, I turn out to be thoroughly pragmatic; I choose hope because I want energy and happiness in my days.

There is so much pleasure as I slice a red-orange tomato, then make each circle into chunks and slide them with their juice into the pan where chopped garlic warms, releasing fragrance, in olive oil and butter. With finger and thumb I pick up a cube I had neglected, and take onto my tongue the soft ripe fruit as twilight lingers outside the kitchen window. I feel the foolishness of my ecstasy in this, yet also the power, and I wonder why so few arrive here, but instead fall for the "joy" of some imagined supremacy, some exclusive thing that is valued precisely because others cannot have it. Then I remember how mortally (and morally) injured we are when we grasp like that, and how despairing. Is it beyond us to know and love ourselves in ways that do not depend on the diminishment of another?

Radical hope does not pretend to know it all, but is curious and thrives on questions. It takes courage, and is healing, to unravel the connections between our religious interpretations and the world's well-being; between what scares us and how we parent our children (or teach our students); between how we feed, shelter, and transport ourselves, and the possibility that all can live well.

To practice radical hope is to proceed as if our lives matter and as if every one of us can contribute in irreplaceable ways to the shared well-being that we have not, after all, forgotten how to desire. It is to feel sharply the grief of not dwelling in the world we want, but also to trust that our actions can bring that world into being, with foretastes for ourselves and feasts for those who come after. Together, from diverse paths, may we dare a deeper, more secure, more sustainable happiness, one that can be handed on—and refashioned—from one generation to the next.

Growing Into God

THIS MORNING, BACK FROM ERRANDS, Michal swept into the house with forsythia, tall branches with bright yellow blooms all over, and put them here beside the desk to cheer me on. She has seedlings growing, too, in a black plastic tray on the cart beside the east kitchen window, slender green shoots with their heads just coming up in today's light. They will be sunflowers. I go back there every once in awhile to look at them. Also to get a bite of chocolate. All day I have had in the back of my mind a passage from the medieval theologian Meister Eckhardt: "The seed of God is in us. Now the seed of a pear tree grows into a pear tree; and a hazel seed grows into a hazel tree; a seed of God grows into God." Alleluia. Jesus is risen. And so am I.

PROVISIONAL PROPOSITIONS

EARLY THIS AFTERNOON AS I DROVE through the woods, sifting through the uninvestigated givens of my faith, I found these: none of us can possibly know God as well as Jesus did; none of us can ever be God as much as Jesus was. I can't remember when I swallowed those two assumptions. No one said I had to. No one spoke them aloud. But some claims become so embedded in a way of believing that they operate without needing to be mentioned. Going unsaid even adds to their power. It removes them from our conversation. It prevents us from recognizing them for what they are—provisional propositions for our journey into joy—to be explored together along the way, and revised or replaced when it helps.

Finally, after all these years, I saw and said those two assumptions out loud. They sounded rude—blunt and bereft of grace. They drew the line. They slammed the door. They disrespected me. Along with everybody else. Including Jesus. Not to mention God. I was offended.

Rolling down the car window, inhaling fresh, spicy waves of sun-warmed air surrounded by miles of pines, I asked myself... What if we can know God just as well as Jesus did? What if we can grow to be God as much as Jesus was? My mouth watered. I began to laugh.

FIFTY-ONE HOLY WEEKS

PERHAPS IT IS NO ACCIDENT THAT WITH this spring's profusion of wildflowers, I am learning to see my struggle to untangle love from domination as sacred work. It is beautiful and healing. It is feminist and mystical, and yes, it is part of my being Christian.

This work, always a challenge, is perhaps most difficult when it comes to finding grounds for hope as I allow myself to know, in depths of my mind and body, that Jesus was murdered. Many interpreters have left the impression that this brutal act of penalty and threat was part of God's plan, and was somehow our fault, and took place for our salvation, and, last but not least, was necessary to open a path to the joy of resurrection, the outpouring of the Holy Spirit, and the fulfillment of justice and peace. I faith-fully repudiate these ways of understanding the torture and killing of Jesus.

It shocks me now that the week of the year when we acknowledge this violence is usually called "Holy Week," as if the holiest things that have ever happened in our faith tradition happened then. I no longer believe this is so. Instead, I believe that the holiest things in Christian tradition happened before the arrest and execution of Jesus and continue to happen whenever people dare to trust divine power, break free from oppression, and know the tremendous pleasure of loving their own lives, each other, and the world.

I know what the Roman oppressors, driven by fear, did to try to stop the healing love of Jesus. I meditate deeply on the tragedy of what the executioners did for one week of each year. I give thanks that divine love never abandoned Jesus, just as it will not leave us alone when we act to make our own healing dreams come true.

But for the fifty-one weeks left over, for the round, sacred span of the rest of each year, I focus my meditation on the life, courage, creativity, humor, justice, and ecstasy of the spiritual movement Jesus belonged to and continues to bless. To honor the power of divine love, so beautifully shown forth in the life of Jesus and so ready to bloom in all our lives, I now observe fifty-one Holy Weeks and one Execution Week in my spiritual year.

EXECUTION EVE

THIS EVENING, A THURSDAY, WHEN tradition commemorates the last meal Jesus had with his friends, I baked a loaf of bread. It was apple bread—easy and moist and sweet. I savored the taste of it in my mouth, received with pleasure the sensation of my stomach becoming full, and gave thanks for the exquisite gift of the beloved friends with whom I share this journey upon the earth. I remembered that Jesus liked to eat and talk and laugh and dream with his friends. I remembered the sweetness of their life together, the passion of how they entered into divine love and healing.

EXECUTION DAY

ON THIS AFTERNOON OF EXECUTION DAY, I have lit a candle here on my desk. I remember that the believers in domination killed Jesus by public crucifixion in order to pursue their purposes of intimidation and control. I now voice my renunciation of any notion that Jesus was killed for me or for God or for salvation or for justice. I remember other persons whose love has been met with violence. I declare my faith that this is not what God wants, that torture is not what makes justice possible, that murder is not what opens the way toward joy. I recall the times I have been threatened and betrayed; the times when my love has been condemned, my life ruled out, my spirit suffocated. In response to all acts of violence, toward Jesus, toward others, and toward myself, I will listen to the truth of my anger and grief and hope. I pray that we all may be liberated from doing violence.

WHEN DOES EASTER COME?

IT IS SATURDAY NIGHT. I SPENT TODAY walking and resting, and then, after supper, Michal and I sat in our kitchen at a card table covered with newspapers and colored Easter eggs.

I remember one Easter morning at St. Mark's Presbyterian in Tucson, when Michal leaned over and whispered, "Look, there's Naomi and Ruth." And there they were, right next to our pew, walking along, beautiful in stained glass, their cloaks golden, their backs toward us, their arms around each other, their road flung out before them, sinking and rising over desert hills, flowing through shadow and light.

Catching sight of them in that moment, I wondered, when does Easter come? Surely not just once. Or only after Jesus. Surely Easter came also to Naomi and Ruth, his long ago grandmothers, as they went out together, shaking off despair, not knowing where their faith would lead. Maybe Easter was bread in their mouths after famine. Maybe Easter was finding friends who believed with them that love can change what is possible. Maybe Easter began as they walked out into the wide world with their arms around each other. In church, that Easter, I leaned over to Michal and whispered, "I love our beautiful road."

Lavender Egg

VERY EARLY THIS EASTER MORNING, I went outdoors to watch the light. I saw new leaves uncurl on the trees around our house and heard the voice of a certain thrasher who has been waking us with spirited songs all spring. I gave thanks for the intimacy of my friendship with Jesus. I remembered that the forces of oppression don't own everything—don't own Jesus, God, love, or me. I sat in the loose-jointed chair beside Saint Francis, cracked open a lavender shell and ate the egg inside, welcoming the mystery of divine power all around and deep within me. Then, yet again, I turned to my heart and listened. Who knows what prayers I will say tomorrow morning? Who can tell what I will learn about love this afternoon?

Advance praise, continued

"... wise, beautiful, brave, and elegant. There is something very beautiful about this book, something that people who are not Christians can read with deep pleasure, for the author's generous sensibility transcends denominational or confessional differences."

Dr. Achsah Guibbory
Professor of English and Religious Studies
University of Illinois
Urbana, Illinois

Youngdahl "seeks to 'untangle love from domination' by fiercely resisting any image of God, Jesus, or Spirit that would stifle joy, diminish self-worth, or dampen desire. She embraces incarnation as a universal human calling, believing that each of us can experience intimacy with God."

The Rev. Dr. Melanie Morrison
Co-Director, The Leaven Center
Lyons, Michigan

"Pat Youngdahl writes with lyrical insight, so elegant in its simplicity and thereby brimming with powerful eloquence, spirit, and richness of theological reflection, from new insights on the meaning of incarnation to a theological reframing of crucifixion and resurrection."

The Rev. Dr. Gail Ricciuti
Associate Professor of Homiletics
Colgate Rochester Crozer Divinity School
Rochester, New York

"Whosoever shall enter into heartfelt communion with this bold, reverent journey shall go forth thoroughly seduced by a divine presence that heals, thrills, nourishes, and promises a fearless love we can carry with us wherever we go."

The Rev. Dr. Sandra A. Szelag
Pastoral Counselor
Tucson, Arizona

These "reflections sing the knowledge that joy and play in ordinary time are both pleasurable and acts of resistance to oppression. For oppressors seek to control and limit such experiences of self-worth. To dance them is truly subversive!"

The Rev. Dr. Peggy Way
Professor of Pastoral Theology
Eden Theological Seminary
St. Louis, Missouri

"... elegant testimony to the Spirit calling us to embody our passion for justice. A delightful book!"

The Rev. Dr. Carter Heyward
Author, Saving Jesus From Those Who Are Right, *and*
God in the Balance: Christian Spirituality
in Times of Terror
Cambridge, Massachusetts

"There is a relentless openness here to divine love, whose presence provides life-giving joy, freedom, and hope in the face of disappointment, pain, and rejection, as well as new ways in which to view the world."

Dr. Dale A. Johnson
Professor of Church History
Vanderbilt Divinity School
Nashville, Tennessee

"... a stunningly beautiful little volume of poetics, prose, and prayers... soul-force in the struggle for a more inclusive church and world."

The Rev. Dr. Deborah Flemister Mullen
Dean of Master's Programs
McCormick Theological Seminary
Chicago, Illinois

Watch for the Subversive Devotions Daily Reader

coming in 2004! For more information, call

BeanPole Books at 888-815-5961.